Kids Talk About
Fairness

by Carrie Finn illustrated by Amy Bailey Muehlenhardt

PICTURE WINDOW BOOKS
Minneapolis, Minnesota

Special thanks to our advisers for their expertise:

Dr. Kay Herting Wahl, Director of School Counseling
University of Minnesota

Susan Kesselring, M.A., Literacy Educator
Rosemount–Apple Valley–Eagan (Minnesota) School District

Editor: Christianne Jones

Designer: Joe Anderson

Page Production: Brandie Shoemaker

Editorial Director: Carol Jones

Creative Director: Keith Griffin

The illustrations in this book were created digitally.

Picture Window Books

5115 Excelsior Boulevard

Suite 232

Minneapolis, MN 55416

877-845-8392

www.picturewindowbooks.com

Printed in the United States of America.

Photo Credit: New York Times Co./Getty Images, page 30

Library of Congress Cataloging-in-Publication Data

Finn, Carrie.

Kids talk about fairness / by Carrie Finn ; illustrated by Amy Bailey Muehlenhardt.

p. cm. – (Kids talk jr.)

Includes bibliographical references and index.

ISBN-13: 978-1-4048-2316-7 (hardcover)

ISBN-10: 1-4048-2316-6 (hardcover)

1. Fairness—Juvenile literature. I. Muehlenhardt, Amy Bailey, 1974- ill. II. Title. III. Series.

BJ1533.F3F56 2007   2006003400

179'.9–dc22

Kids Talk Jr.

COUNSELOR: Sam

Hi, Friends!

My name is Sam Strong. I'm in the fifth grade at Eagle Elementary. I really like helping my friends with their problems. My friends call me "Super Sam the Problem Solver."

Lots of kids like you have sent me questions about fairness. When things are fair, they are even or equal. Read on and see the advice that I give about fairness.

Sincerely,

Sam

Dear Sam,

My brother got a new bike for his birthday. I want a new bike, but I have to wait until my birthday. Why can't I just have a new bike now?

Jed

Kids Talk Jr.

COUNSELOR: Sam

Dear Jed,

You need to be patient. Part of being fair is waiting your turn for a gift. Your birthday will come soon enough.

Sam

Dear Sam,

Why do I have to go to bed earlier than my big sister?

Keisha

Kids Talk Jr.

COUNSELOR: Sam

Dear Keisha,

I'm sure your big sister had an earlier bedtime when she was your age. Your parents have to be fair with the rules. When you get to be as old as your big sister is now, your bedtime will probably be later, too.

Sam

Dear Sam,

At recess my friend got mad because I was on the swing, but it was my turn. What should I do?

Tory

Kids Talk Jr.

COUNSELOR: Sam

Dear Tory,

My teacher let us swing for five minutes each. Then we had to switch. Tell your friend that when your turn is up, you will be happy to share the swing with him.

Sam

11

Dear Sam,

My teacher said that boys and girls haven't always been treated the same. What was she talking about?

Lilly

Kids Talk Jr.

COUNSELOR: Sam

Dear Lilly,

Years ago, girls weren't allowed to play sports. Then laws were created to make sure that there was equality between boys and girls. Things have changed a lot since then.

Sam

Dear Sam,

How can I be fair when I am playing with more than one friend?

Tyler

Kids Talk Jr.

COUNSELOR: Sam

Dear Tyler,

You can be patient when you are waiting for your turn. You can also make sure everyone is included in a game. Your friends will appreciate your willingness to be fair.

Sam

Dear Sam,

I can invite only two friends to the zoo with me, but I have more friends than that. Who should I invite?

Dawson

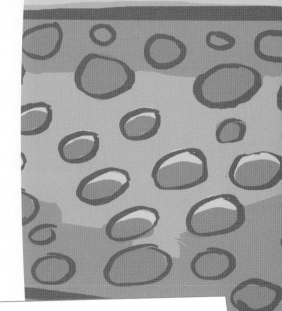

Kids Talk Jr.

COUNSELOR: Sam

Dear Dawson,

My mom said that you should invite two of your closest friends this time. Next time, invite some other friends. That's the best way to be fair.

Sam

Dear Sam,

My dad paid me $5 to wash his car. Do I have to give some of the money to my sister since she helped?

Leo

Kids Talk Jr.

COUNSELOR: Sam

Dear Leo,

Just because your dad gave you the money doesn't mean that you shouldn't be fair. Give your sister part of the money for helping you do the work.

Sam

Dear Sam,

My friend Polly uses a wheelchair and wants to play basketball with me. How can we make the game fair?

Cameron

Kids Talk Jr.

COUNSELOR: Sam

Dear Cameron,

Because Polly uses a wheelchair, the rules might have to change a bit. You and Polly should set up some new rules together. This way, the game will be fair to both of you.

Sam

Dear Sam,

I got a new puppy. My mom told me that everyone in the family has to take care of him. How are we going to do that?

Keenan

Kids Talk Jr.

COUNSELOR: Sam

Dear Keenan,

Your mom wants to make sure that everyone shares equal responsibility for the puppy. You should all sit down and come up with a list of what needs to be done. Figure out who is going to do each task so it's fair.

Sam

24

Dear Sam,

My friends want me to decide who gets to use the computer next. What should I do?

Gracie

Kids Talk Jr.

COUNSELOR: Sam

Dear Gracie,

You could draw numbers to see who goes next. Then, make sure everyone has equal time on the computer. Maybe you could find a computer game you could all play together.

Sam

Kids Talk Jr.

COUNSELOR: Sam

That's all the time I have for today. I have to meet some friends at the skate park. I hope I answered all of your questions about being fair. There is plenty more to read about. Turn the page and learn more about fairness.

Sincerely,

Sam

Grab a piece of paper and a pencil, and take this fun quiz. Good luck!

1. Being patient means
   a) waiting until it's your birthday to get a gift.
   b) jumping up and down, and crying until you get a gift.
   c) complaining every day about not getting a gift.

2. The older you get
   a) the more fish you have to catch.
   b) the later you get to stay up at night.
   c) the fewer books you will read.

3. To be fair at recess
   a) only boys should be allowed to swing on the swings.
   b) only girls should be allowed to swing on the swings.
   c) everyone should get a turn to swing on the swings.

4. Boys and girls were treated differently
   a) on television.
   b) many years ago.
   c) on Thursdays.

5. When you are fair, you will
   a) not let anyone play with your toys.
   b) not let everyone have a turn at bat.
   c) do your best to include everyone.

6. If you can bring only two friends with you to the zoo, to be fair you should
   a) invite two people but make sure to invite other people next time.
   b) invite only the people who buy you presents.
   c) go alone.

7. When your sister helps you wash the car, you should
   a) keep the money for yourself.
   b) be fair and give her some of the money.
   c) spend the money right away so you don't have to share.

8. The rules to basketball can be changed to be more fair
   a) if your friend uses a wheelchair and wants to play with you.
   b) if you ask your teacher first.
   c) when it's raining outside.

9. When you get a new puppy, you will want to
   a) wash him with soap and water before you take him outside.
   b) share the responsibilities of taking care of him.
   c) feed him only bananas and brussels sprouts.

10. Using the computer fairly means
    a) everyone uses it at once.
    b) only one person can play.
    c) friends can take turns playing, or they can play together.

Jackie Robinson

Jackie Robinson grew up when some places had separate schools, separate restaurants, and separate bathrooms for people who were black and white. Many people, including Jackie, thought that these rules weren't fair.

Jackie was hired to play baseball for the Brooklyn Dodgers. He became the first black man to play Major League Baseball. Many people didn't think it was OK for a black baseball player to play with white baseball players. Some players and fans were mean to Jackie.

Jackie never gave up. He helped his team win many games. He led them to winning the World Series in 1955.

Jackie showed everyone how important it was to treat all people with fairness, no matter what color skin they have.

Glossary

advice—suggestions about what to do about a problem

appreciate—to value someone or something

equal—when things are exactly the same

equality—being equal

patient—to act calm while waiting your turn

responsibility—showing that you can take care of something

willingness—ready to do something

To Learn More

AT THE LIBRARY

Bender, Marie. *Fairness Counts.* Edina, Minn.: Abdo Pub., 2003.

Kyle, Kathryn. *Fairness.* Chanhassen, Minn.: Child's World, 2003.

Small, Mary. *Being Fair.* Minneapolis: Picture Window Books, 2006.

ON THE WEB

FactHound offers a safe, fun way to find Internet sites related to this book.

All of the sites on FactHound have been researched by our staff.

1. Visit *www.facthound.com*

2. Type in this special code for age-appropriate sites: 1404823166

3. Click on the **FETCH IT** button.

Your trusty FactHound will fetch the best sites for you!

Index

Look for all of the books in the Kids Talk Jr. series:

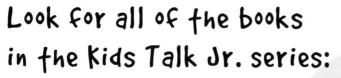